"I am grateful for books that help bring the true story of the Bible into the everyday spaces of a child's life. This does that so wonderfully well!"

KRISTYN GETTY, Songwriter and Author

"The story of Zacchaeus is a wonderful story of the changed heart and life that believing the gospel requires and that trusting in Jesus brings. Carl Laferton has done a wonderful job of communicating these truths to children and parents. Make sure to add this book to your collection of Tales That Tell the Truth!"

CONNIE DEVER, Capitol Hill Baptist Church, Washington, D.C.

"I love this book, and I love the story of Zacchaeus. We need to give every child this story to show them that Jesus came for every child. As you read this with your kids, they'll see and feel what a joy it is to belong to Jesus."

ED DREW, Founder, Faith in Kids; Author,
Raising Confident Kids in a Confusing World

thegoodbook
for children

The Man in the Tree and the Brand New Start
© The Good Book Company / Catalina Echeverri 2024.

Illustrated by Catalina Echeverri | Design & Art Direction by André Parker

"The Good Book For Children" is an imprint of The Good Book Company Ltd
North America: thegoodbook.com UK: thegoodbook.co.uk Australia: thegoodbook.com.au
New Zealand: thegoodbook.co.nz India: thegoodbook.co.in

ISBN: 9781784989644 | JOB-007774 | Printed in India

Carl LAFERTON

Catalina ECHEVERRI

THE MAN in the TREE AND THE BRAND NEW START

There are three things you
need to Know about Zacchaeus.

Number one: Zacchaeus was very short.
Whenever he went to the market in Jericho,
he was the smallest grown-up there.

Number two:
Zacchaeus was very rich.

Whenever he
went to the
market, he
was the richest
grown-up there.

In fact, Zacchaeus wanted, more than anything, to be richer.

His job was to take money from people in Jericho and give it to their rulers.

But Zacchaeus would take extra money from people... and keep it for himself. Zacchaeus wanted to be rich more than he wanted to be kind or to obey God.

But... Number three: even though he was rich, Zacchaeus was not very happy.

Whenever he went to the market, he could buy anything he wanted — but that wasn't making him happy.

One day, this small, rich, not-very-happy man noticed a crowd gathering along the road outside his house. What was going on?

"Jesus is coming through Jericho on his way to Jerusalem!" someone said.

Jesus? Zacchaeus had heard about him.

Jesus said
amazing things.

Jesus did
amazing things.

Most amazingly of all,
people said Jesus was God
himself, who had come to
rule his people and put
wrong things right.

Suddenly Zacchaeus wanted, more
than anything, to see Jesus.

But he had a problem.

The crowds were big. Zacchaeus was small. And no one was going to help him see Jesus, because no one wanted to help a man who took what wasn't his.

But Zacchaeus wanted,
more than anything,
to see Jesus.

He ran along the road.
He saw a sycamore tree.

And he made a plan.

but he was going
to see Jesus!

It was hard,
because he
was short —

Up he
climbed.

Zacchaeus peered over the crowd.
Jesus was coming! He reached
the tree. And then...

Jesus stopped.

Looked up.

And spoke...

"Zacchaeus, come down straight away.
I would like to stay at your house today."

Zacchaeus looked down.
Jesus was being kind to... him?
Jesus wanted to be friends
with... him? Even though he
cared about money more than
being kind or obeying God?

Yes!

Down he climbed. It was hard, because he was short — but he was going to speak to Jesus!

"Thank you, Jesus," he said. "I would love to have you come to my house."

So off they went. Zacchaeus was going to spend time with Jesus! For the first time that he could remember, deep down inside he was feeling... happy!

But the crowd was very *not* happy.

"Wait, what?"

"Why is Jesus going
to *his* house?"

"Zacchaeus takes money for
himself. He doesn't care about
being kind. He doesn't obey God.
Why does Jesus want to be
friends with him?"

Then Zacchaeus spoke to Jesus and said something that no one in Jericho, including Zacchaeus, would ever have imagined he'd say.

"Lord," he said, which was his way of saying that Jesus was his ruler now.

"I am going to give half of everything I own to people who don't have much.

"And I know I have taken money that I shouldn't have. I am going to give those people four times more than I took from them."

Wait, what?!

What had changed between Zacchaeus climbing up that tree and coming down that tree?

He had met Jesus.

Jesus had shown him a love he didn't expect.
Jesus had shown him a Kindness he didn't deserve.

So now Zaccheus did not want more money.

Now he just wanted to love Jesus.

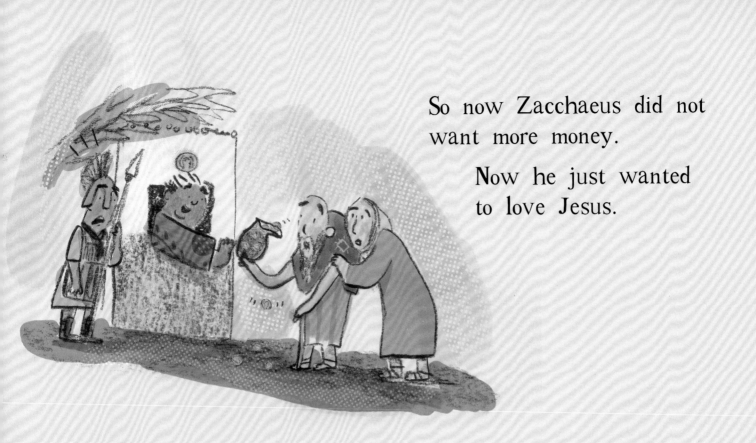

Now Zacchaeus didn't want to get more for himself.
Now he wanted to be kind with what he had.

Then Jesus spoke.

"Today Zacchaeus
has a new start
with God – a
new start that
will last for ever
and ever."

"I came to find and save lost people like Zacchaeus — people who know they have got things wrong in life."

That's why Jesus was going *through* Jericho *to* Jerusalem.

He was going to do all that so that he could put wrong things right and give people like Zacchaeus a new start that would last for ever.

He was going to Jerusalem to die
on a cross, and rise again to life,
and go home to heaven to rule.

So now there are three things you need to Know about Zacchaeus.

He was still short.

He was a lot poorer.

But now he was a lot, lot happier, and he was a lot, lot Kinder...

because he Knew that Jesus loved him, and he loved Jesus — and that made all the difference.

The Bible says that everyone
is like Zacchaeus was.

Sometimes we take what
isn't ours.

Sometimes we want, more
than anything, to have
more things.

Sometimes we don't care about being Kind,
and we don't obey God.

Jesus says to us,

"I came to find and save you.
I would like to be your Lord and your
friend today and every day, on into forever."

Like Zacchaeus, all we need to do is say...

"Thank you, Jesus.
I'm sorry that I have not always obeyed you.
I want to live with you as my Lord.
I would love to be your friend."

And then...

You might be
short or tall.

You might be rich or poor.

But you can be happy deep down inside because you know the Lord Jesus loves you.

And you can be kind and you can live how Jesus says because, more than anything, you love Jesus.

Just like Zacchaeus.

TALES that Tell the TRUTH

HOW DO WE KNOW ABOUT
THE MAN IN THE TREE AND THE BRAND NEW START?

The true story of Jesus and Zacchaeus (and the tree) is told in the Bible in Luke 19 v 1-10. It takes place near the end of Jesus' journey to Jerusalem, the capital city of Judea. Jesus knew that when he reached Jerusalem, he would be killed on a cross before rising back to life again (Luke 18 v 31-33).

Zacchaeus was the last of lots of different people that Jesus met on his way to Jerusalem. And Zacchaeus shows us how *we* should respond to Jesus. We watch Zacchaeus *repent*: he changes his mind about who is in charge of his life. At the start of the story, he is in charge and getting more money is what he most wants to do. It doesn't make him very happy! By the end of the story, Jesus is in charge of Zacchaeus, and living Jesus' way is what Zacchaeus most wants to do. This is what Jesus calls all of us to do — to "repent and believe the good news" (Mark 1 v 15). When we understand the good news that Jesus is God's Son and that he loves us, we can joyfully live with him as our Lord, obeying his commands and knowing we are forgiven. Being followers of Jesus makes a wonderful difference to our hearts and to our lives — just as it did to Zacchaeus's.

Enjoy all of the award-winning "Tales That Tell The Truth" series:

www.thegoodbook.com | .co.uk